Flora and Tiger
19 very short stories
from my life

Flora and Tiger

19 very short stories
from my life

Flora and Tiger
19 very short stories
from my life
Eric Carle

SCHOLASTIC INC.

New York Toronto London Auckland Sydney
Mexico City New Delhi Hong Kong

Contents

Stories that took place in America are in red.
Stories that took place in Germany are in blue.

To My Readers

Every so often children who have grown up enjoying my picture books ask me whether I wrote or planned to write "older" books. "Have you written any real books?" someone wrote to me.

Inspired by my questioners, I have written *Flora and Tiger*. The events in these stories take place from my earliest childhood to the present. They tell of things that happened when I lived in the United States where I was born, in Germany where I grew up, and in the United States again where I have lived and worked since 1952.

All of these stories are true. But I set them down, not in the order in which they occurred, but as they came to me.

For readers who would like to know what took place when, a few notes about my life may be useful. I was born in 1929 in the United States to German immigrant parents. When I was six years old, my mother and father returned to Germany, where I received most of my education.

When I was ten years old, World War II (1939-1945) broke out, and on the first day of that war, my father was drafted into the German army. Stuttgart, where I lived, and other German cities became the bombing targets of the Allied air forces, and in 1943, my schoolmates and I, together with our teachers, were evacuated to a small town near the Swiss border to be protected from the bombings. Except for an occasional furlough, I did not see my father again, until I was an eighteen-year-old art student, when he returned from a prisoner-of-war camp inside the Soviet Union, a changed and broken man.

The stories in this book, from various places and times of my life, have three things in common: animals or insects, friends or relatives, and me.

My father loved animals, it is from him that I inherited that love for all kinds of creatures. My father liked to draw, it is from him that I inherited the joy of picture making. My father was a storyteller, it is from him that I learned to tell a story. These stories are for him, with gratitude and love.

With my father, when I was six years old

My Father, My Teacher

Often on his days off from work, my father would take me for long walks. Not far from our house we walked along a brook with old willow trees overhanging its banks. We lifted up pieces of rotten bark to expose beetles, centipedes and grubs. In the wet grass we might discover a black-and-orange salamander; I'd hold the moist creature in the palm

of my hand to study it before returning the salamander to where we had found it. We poked at smooth stones in the gurgling water to see a fish dash away. A startled frog might jump from the embankment.

One day, farther away from the brook, between meadow and forest, we carefully touched an anthill to see the ants rush out to defend and repair their nest.

"This was once an empty spot," my father said. "But on a warm summer day an ant queen flew in and landed here. She decided it was a good place to settle; it was dry and it had a southern exposure; the sun would keep it warm all day long." As he spoke, his bushy eyebrows rose and fell.

"After the queen landed she bit off her wings. They had served her on her one and only flight; thereafter they would be useless. Then she dug into the soil or underneath a small rock and started laying eggs. In the beginning she had to feed herself, but soon each egg developed into a larva, and each larva into an ant. As soon as these ants grow up, it will be their job to feed the queen. From then on the queen will be only an egg-laying machine until she dies, years from now."

I would imagine the poor queen, deep inside the ever-growing ant colony, never to see the sun again. When I looked closer all I saw were busy ants rushing about, carrying food (a dead caterpillar, for instance), repairing and building the anthill. None of them seemed either happy or unhappy, and I assumed that the queen, too, simply did her job.

"Almost all eggs turn into sterile female ants who will be unable to lay eggs of their own," my father explained. "Their only purpose is to feed and groom the queen, to care for the young, to build the anthill and keep it in good repair."

How selfless, I thought.

"Only when the queen is old and dies, or when the colony becomes too big will a new queen emerge," my father went on. "Sometimes a young strong queen ant may enter the anthill from outside and kill the older, weaker queen. Or a new queen may be raised inside the colony. Eventually she, too, will eliminate the old one."

How cruel, I thought.

We continued our walk and entered the silent forest. We walked on the soft path and stepped across exposed roots.

"See the hole underneath that old oak tree," my father pointed out. "That's a fox den." He examined the ground near the entrance of the den. "If the ground is worn and no grass or plants grow near the entrance, a fox is going in and out. This one seems empty. I even see some spiderwebs; they wouldn't last long if a fox were entering and leaving."

And I held onto his hand. I still remember the touch and shape of his hand, the hair on its back, the bluish veins, his neat fingernails with the white half-moons at their base.

As we stepped out of the forest, we reached our destination: the *Schloss Solitude*, a castle on top of a hill with views far across the land. We sat quietly in the grass for a while to enjoy the vistas and then began our journey home. At the bottom of the hill we stopped at the *Muckenstüble* (Room of Flies), a peasant inn. I ordered a *Schmalzbrot*, pieces of onion

and slices of apple that had been fried in lard, making a mixture that tasted delicious when spread on dark rye bread.

Looking through the window of the inn, my father discovered a nest of swallows underneath the eaves of the barn. "Look, look." He pointed. And it didn't take long before father and son were watching the swift birds soar through the air to catch flies. Every so often a swallow disappeared into the nest to feed its young, who were begging with tiny, insistent chirping noises.

The waitress, wearing a black dress and white apron, added up our bill. My father paid and we left, taking with us a few pieces of bread from the table to be fed to a pair of black swans and their young in a nearby pond.

My Oma, She-Goat and Chicken

My Opa, my mother's father, bought a four-story brick house that had been built at the turn of the century. Each floor had a living room, two bedrooms and a kitchen. Before long, my Opa's children and their families moved in to fill up all four floors. My parents and I lived on the second floor.

Behind the house stood an old wooden structure in which a *Küfer*, a barrelmaker, had once conducted his business.

My Opa rebuilt the barrelmaker's shop into a small factory that produced parts for Porsche cars. Several large presses operated by men and women stamped out thousands of disks, plates and other metal parts. Once a week a truck from the nearby Porsche factory pulled up to my Opa's factory and picked up these parts.

When the presses went "thump-thump-thump," my Opa would say, *"Ein Pfennig-ein Pfennig-ein Pfennig,"* a penny-a penny-a penny. And, a penny at a time, my Opa eventually became quite well-to-do.

Both my Opa and my Oma, my mother's mother, had come from peasant families. At the age of fourteen or fifteen each had left their poor parents and siblings and moved to the Big City. My Oma became a maid and worked for a wealthy family. My Opa apprenticed himself to a tinsmith. Soon their lives crossed and they married. They had seven children, of whom five survived.

I never heard them complain about the poverty of their early lives on the farm. In fact, they always retained a certain longing and fondness for the land and especially for farm animals.

Behind the factory was a narrow strip of open space. Here my grandparents built a small wooden shed that soon housed several chickens and a she-goat. Inside the shed the chickens cackled and the goat bleated, competing with the powerful thumps of the presses inside the factory.

In the evening, the animals were let out of the shed so that the chickens could scratch and pick among the gravel and grasses and the goat could exercise. The chickens rarely strayed, but the goat, curious and rambunctious, loved nothing more than to visit my Oma. The goat would dash into the house, climb three flights of stairs and knock with

her forehead on my Oma's door, begging for a special treat, a handful of oats or a green leaf from the small indoor garden that my Oma grew on the veranda next to the kitchen.

Some of the family members then watched the animals to make sure that they didn't stray toward the street.

One evening it was my turn to keep an eye on the chickens and the goat. As I watched I got bored. And when I got bored, I decided to do some mischief.

I loved my Oma. I adored my Oma. But I was also young and not beyond playing a trick on her.

I took a chicken and gently laid it on its back, feet skyward. At the same time I placed my other hand soothingly over the chicken's head, covering its eyes as I bent its head slowly flat against the ground. For about half a minute I calmly kept one hand on the chicken's body, the other hand over its head. Then I removed my hands.

The chicken would not jump up. No, it would remain on its back without so much as a twitch. Thousands of years ago when chickens still lived in the wild, they "played dead" in order to fool a fox or weasel about to attack. A fox or a weasel would often lose interest in a bird that did not fly, run, jump, wiggle, dart or hop. I had merely taken advantage of the chicken's instinct to fool my Oma.

After I had laid out all of her four chickens in a row, I rang my Oma's bell. When she looked out of her window, I pointed excitedly at the lifeless-looking chickens. Jumping up and down with my arms flailing, I pretended something terrible had happened.

It worked! In no time my Oma had raced downstairs and stood in the doorway pale and bewildered, unable to move or even to cry.

I then walked calmly up to the lifeless chickens, bent down and clapped my hands as hard as I could. Startled, the chickens jumped up, ruffled their feathers and resumed their picking and scratching as if nothing had happened.

My Oma walked over to me, took me by the ear and led me up the stairs to her kitchen. But did she punish me? No, she prepared hot cocoa for me and served it with one of her homemade cookies.

You can see why my Oma was special.

A Mother Bird and Her Young

Three sides of the house where I live in the summer are surrounded by the forest. Through the trees on a long and slightly uphill driveway you approach what I call the front but what my wife calls the back of the house. On the fourth side of the house is a wooden deck enclosed by a stone wall. This wall is the home of quick chipmunks and sluggish hornets.

From the deck you can see a meadow stretch gradually downhill for about two hundred yards to a point where the grass abruptly ends and the forest begins. Abruptly is an exaggeration because there is a narrow band, four or so feet wide, a kind of no-man's-land that in a fuzzy way divides the two areas.

Every spring I hack away at the saplings and low bushes that grow in this no-man's-land, trying to achieve a clean line separating the grass from the trees. It must be my upbringing, the need to line things up, to establish orderliness, that compels me to do this year after year. So far, neither I nor that narrow band between meadow and forest has permanently succeeded in winning the struggle.

Last spring, as I was again clearing the growth in that narrow strip, I lopped off a sapling with one swift chop of my hatchet. The young tree was perhaps five feet tall and an inch thick at its base. As it fell I noticed a bird's nest in the fork of the branches; from it three small eggs rolled onto the grass.

What to do? I lifted the sapling and, with my hatchet, sharpened the base to a point, as one would sharpen a pencil with a pocketknife. I stuck it firmly back into the ground. Then I picked up the three eggs and placed them back inside the nest.

After a while, the mother bird returned to the *replanted* tree, ruffled her feathers and hopped into her nest. The next day, my wife and I watched from a distance. We noticed that the leaves had begun to wilt but the bird sat in her nest, patiently hatching the three little eggs. The following day the leaves had shriveled up, and the day after that they turned brown and dropped to the ground. But the mother bird remained at her post, leaving only for short periods to feed herself.

The barren tree and the exposed nest looked pitiful

against the lush green background. The bird and the nest were now exposed to the sun, rain and an occasional thunderstorm. A fox from below or a hawk flying in circles above could easily spot the unlucky bird. This perilous situation, however, did not deter her from her duty.

Every morning, with the first rays of the rising sun, my wife and I looked toward the forlorn tree and the bird on her nest. One day, we saw that the eggs had hatched. The mother bird's task was halfway completed, but now she had to feed her brood. In this she was as unfaltering as she had been in hatching the eggs. Every time, when she flew toward her nest, the young birds chirped and chattered until they had been fed; then the mother flew away again.

Before long, the young birds took their flying lessons, first jumping from nest to branch, then from branch to branch, until finally, one by one, they flew to a neighboring tree. It wasn't long before mother and children disappeared into the green foliage of the forest.

At the end of the year I removed the dead sapling. The now deserted nest was still in its place but by now it had a rather forlorn look.

Hen or Rooster?

Food was scarce during the war and groceries could be bought only with food stamps. For this reason my grandparents kept chickens for eggs and rabbits for an occasional Sunday roast.

These animals were kept in the garden behind my grandparents' house. My grandfather, my father's father, had built a henhouse next to the cherry tree and then put a wire fence around it all. About half a dozen chickens and a proud rooster pecked among the grass and weeds under the tree. After some time, however, the grass disappeared, and after some more time the soil hardened altogether, and the cherry tree began to look sickly.

Whenever I could, I gathered grasses, dandelions and clover from an empty lot across the street and stuffed them all through the fence to feed the chickens. Running from all corners, they eagerly pecked at my offering until it had been gobbled up. Then, their heads cocked sideways, they looked at me for more.

Every so often a hen announced with a "cluck-cluck" her intention to lay an egg and then disappeared into the henhouse. Inside, several boxes filled with straw had been nailed to the wall. Into one of these boxes the hen would lay an egg. Encouraged by the first hen's activity, another hen might start to cluck and, nestling into the next box, would lay an egg as well. That way, there was a constant supply of eggs, more in summer, fewer in winter.

Sometimes my grandmother would put a couple of eggs into a paper bag.

"Here, take them to your mother and tell her to make a pancake for you," she'd say as she pressed the bag into my hand.

One particular chicken was the subject of an ongoing disagreement between my grandparents. My grandmother said it was a hen; my grandfather claimed it was a rooster.

"I heard him crow this morning," he would say defiantly.

In peacetime my grandfather had been a rather stout man but now, several years into the war, he had lost weight. He was always hungry, like everyone else.

"And I just saw her lay an egg," my grandmother would counter.

All their lives my grandparents had relished a good argument, and this was no time to hold back.

Then one day the hen/rooster died of old age and my grandmother buried her/him inside the compost heap in the garden.

A few hours later my grandmother was surprised to find my grandfather in the kitchen with the very same bird. He had carefully plucked it—there were feathers all over the kitchen—cut it into pieces and was stirring it in a pot of boiling hot water.

"But this chicken has died," scolded my grandmother. "You can't eat such a thing!"

"Freshly died is just like butchered," maintained my grandfather, and he kept stirring. He fried some potatoes, placed them alongside the boiled hen/rooster and ate the cooked bird all by himself.

Afterward, every so often my grandparents argued about that bird. My grandfather maintained it had been a rooster, my grandmother that it had been a hen.

Naturally with the evidence gone, they never resolved their disagreement.

Snake

At the age of twenty-one, my father emigrated from Germany to America and settled in Syracuse, N.Y. Two years later his nineteen-year-old sweetheart followed him, and within a year they were married to each other.

My young parents belonged to a group of nature lovers who had a camp near one of the five Finger Lakes. On weekends and during their vacation time, when the weather was hot and humid, they left the city to join their friends. The camp consisted of several log cabins, situated at the edge of the woods near the lake.

After I was born, I was taken along to camp with them. An old photograph shows me as a tiny baby in the arms of my father, who is wearing shorts and has windblown hair. Later, when I was perhaps three years old, someone took a picture of me sitting on a swing, my feet not quite reaching the ground. Next to me, with one hand holding the rope of the swing, stands my beautiful mother, about twenty-four

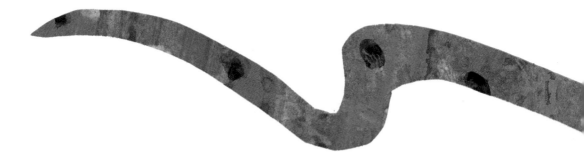

years old. I believe that at that moment I loved my mother as much as ever in my life.

At night, through the open window of the log cabin, I watched moonlit clouds with ragged shadows drifting across a sky studded with millions of stars. I then felt everything was peaceful and secure. But on a cloudy night, when I saw only the black sky, I was overcome by loneliness and fear.

Even as a young boy I enjoyed solitude. One hot, quiet afternoon I wandered off by myself into the forest, away from the campers. The only sound disturbing the stillness was that of my bare feet shuffling through the dry leaves on the ground. Suddenly I noticed a large snake curled up and sunning herself on a ledge. I moved nearer the speckled creature. Her tongue darted back and forth, and the sun flickered in her black eyes, which were turned toward me.

Slowly I put my hand around her smooth, dry body. The snake slithered between my fingers, across my palm, around my hand and toward my elbow. This was the first time I had held a snake—I was surprised by her strength. Using my other hand to hold onto her, I ran through the forest toward the older campers. I wanted to show them what I had found. I wanted to be admired and praised. Instead, some of the campers fled, panic-stricken, while others, paralyzed with fright, stared wide-eyed at me and the snake.

You see, I had not known that some snakes are poisonous. Now my father stepped forward.

"Don't be afraid," explained my father. "It's just a harmless garter snake."

Only then did everyone calm down.

Together, my father and I, snake in hand, walked back among the trees. Near the ledge where I had picked up the snake, my father asked me to release her. Without a sound my snake vanished into the leaves.

My Opa, Bees and Ants

The small tool and die factory my Opa had founded was very successful. After a few years he had made his youngest son, Rudolf, a partner. "Karl and Rudolf Oelschläger, Tool and Die Maker," a sign proclaimed.

My Opa was not only a businessman, he was a philosopher of sorts. I remember him telling me about the life that goes on inside a block of steel. Perhaps I was too young to understand him; perhaps he was talking about atoms and molecules. But metal and machines meant nothing to me.

Unfortunately my uncle Rudolf also had little interest in metal and machines, instead preferring gambling casinos, causing my Opa sleepless nights. So, my Opa began to pin his hopes on me, even though I was only ten or eleven years old.

"Become an engineer," he'd say. "I'll pay for your studies. Then later you can take over the factory."

But as I said, I was not in love with metal and machines. I wanted to become an artist.

Next he wanted me to be a musician. One day a moving van pulled up and, to my surprise, several strong men carried a piano to my room.

"Take piano lessons. I'll pay for them," my Opa said.

A year later, after I had refused to take advantage of his offer, the moving truck reappeared and the piano was removed from my room.

Then it occurred to my Opa that I should become a physician.

"*Herr Doktor*' has a nice ring to it, don't you think?"

But I declined.

"You are lazy and you will amount to nothing."

So I locked myself into his bedroom and in a fit of frustrated anger began to tear down the wallpaper!

"Come out! Or else!" my Opa threatened. But I took my time, finished the job, unlocked the door and marched by my Opa, who was for once, speechless with surprise.

After that he gave up on me. But that is not the story I set out to tell.

My Opa had strange views about food and medicine. For instance, he said vinegar was bad for you. For every drop of vinegar swallowed you'd lose one drop of blood. In goes the vinegar, out goes the blood.

Weird. Maybe I misunderstood his thoughts about vinegar as much as I had about the life inside a block of steel.

Also, he always had his beer served lukewarm. "Cold beer will give you stomach cancer," he claimed.

My Opa had arthritis in his hands. His finger joints were swollen and he complained that they hurt when he moved his fingers.

For this ailment, he had his own peculiar remedy. In front of the house was a narrow garden, surrounded by a picket fence. There were rosebushes and other flowers, and bees everywhere.

My Opa would pick up a bee with his bare fingers and keep the insect inside his rolled-up fist until it stung. He'd repeat this procedure several times with different bees. The bees' poison acted as a painkiller, he insisted.

In the nearby forest there were large anthills, some as much as two or three feet high. These anthills were made of pine needles that the ants had collected and piled up. Millions of large, fierce ants crawled inside their nest and over the surface.

My Opa would place his arthritic hands flat against the anthill. The alarmed ants swarmed over his hands and bit him relentlessly, releasing some kind of poison. I can still recall the sour smell given off by these insects. My Opa swore that this treatment also relieved his pain.

Perhaps the bees' stings and the ants' bites caused greater pain than the arthritis. Or perhaps my Opa was right, and mysterious medicinal ingredients in the stings and bites had magical healing powers.

But perhaps he wasn't.

Maikäfer

When I arrived in Germany from the United States as an English-speaking six-year-old boy, I quickly learned to speak the German language from my German playmates. At first I picked up words, and then sentences. And I also learned about *Maikäfer. Mai* means May in German, and *Käfer*, bug or beetle.

Maikäfer are mainly brown, about an inch long, handsome and slow-moving. All of their six long legs are rough, and perfectly suited to clinging to anything, especially your skin, hair and clothing. I also recall their distinctive feelers. Those of the males are larger than those of the females.

These beetles appear in the forest every May, early if the weather is warm, later if it is cool, and immediately begin to eat tons of oak and beech leaves. They live only for a few weeks or a month, then become sluggish and die, but not before the females have laid their eggs into the ground. These eggs develop into grubs; in four years they grow into mature *Maikäfer* and start the cycle all over again.

It requires enormous effort for *Maikäfer* to fly; first they have to pump themselves up, literally sucking air into special receptacles in their bodies, making themselves airworthy. Awkwardly they fold back the hard wings, then unfold the soft wings underneath, and finally buzz noisily away. All this takes a long time, time enough to enable small children to catch them with great ease.

Every year in early May, my friends and I collected boxes, cigar boxes being the most desired, and drilled small air holes into the lids. We showed our boxes to each other and discussed in detail the pros and cons of this or that box, all the while recounting last year's *Maikäfer* stories.

Then, sure enough, one day the first *Maikäfer* was spotted. This was the signal for us to take our boxes and hurry into the nearby forest.

First you'd place fresh green leaves inside your box,

also a small twig for the beetle to crawl on. In this procedure, too, you needed to be an expert. There had to be enough green leaves for the bugs to feed on, but not too many because the *Maikäfer* also needed room to move around.

It was easy to collect the bugs. They were all over, in the branches, on the bark, in the air, on the ground, on yourself. And, pretty soon, in your box.

You learned to hold the beetle on its side with your thumb and index finger, not allowing its raspy feet to get hold of you. If you held the box quietly near your ear, you could hear the beetles crunch the leaves; if you shook the box even slightly, you heard a loud, protesting buzz.

After a while we'd count how many beetles each of us had caught, and how many males and how many females. If you had more females, then you'd trade with a friend who had more males. Why this was so important to us, I can't remember.

Late in the day, we put our boxes under our arms, took a fistful of fresh oak and beech leaves, and straggled back home, walking along the brook and willow trees.

With pride, I showed the *Maikäfer* collection to my parents. And before I went to bed I cleaned out the box— the beetles produced large, round dung balls—and added fresh fodder for these very hungry creatures.

I placed my box close to my pillow, and before I fell asleep, listening to my beetles munching the leaves, I whispered an old children's rhyme:

> *Maikäfer flieg*
> *Dein Vater ist im Krieg*
> *Deine Mutter ist im Pommerland*
> *Pommerland ist abgebrannt*
> *Maikäfer flieg.*

> *Maikäfer* fly
> Your father is in the war
> Your mother is in Pomerania (a state in eastern Germany)
> Pomerania is burnt to the ground
> *Maikäfer* fly

A year or two later, World War II broke out. My father became a soldier. By the end of the war, half of Stuttgart, where we had been living, was burnt to the ground.

Fifi and the String Bean

In my mid thirties, I moved to Greenwich Village in New York City, and lived there for the next ten years in a formerly elegant brownstone house on Twelfth Street. My walk-up apartment was on the fourth floor. A narrow staircase led all the way up to my place on the top. Each step creaked as you stepped on it. When I first moved in, I feared that the sagging stairs might collapse. But soon I became accustomed to the sounds and motions of every step.

The front room of my apartment was very big, with an enormous skylight that faced north. Here I lived and worked. A narrow hallway led to two bedrooms that overlooked backyard gardens. An old sycamore tree had grown from below past the bedroom windows. Off the hallway were a small kitchen with a noisy refrigerator and a bathroom that had a worn, black-and-white tile floor.

All this I shared with Fifi and Mitzi, my cats. Fifi was a black, long-haired cat; curious and nervous, she had lively round green eyes. Mitzi, a tiger cat, was placid; he often spent hours sleeping on top of the narrow railing of the fire escape. This delicate balancing act four floors above the yard alarmed me at first, but Mitzi's surefootedness soon put me at ease.

One evening I was in my kitchen preparing string beans for my dinner when I noticed Fifi's avid interest in what I was doing. She meowed softly, her green eyes followed my every move, and her tail twitched. I washed the string beans, removed the strings from their seams , snapped them in two and placed them into a bowl.

Then, because Fifi seemed so intent on what I was doing, I bent down and held out a string bean to her. She meowed some more and rose on her hind feet to sniff the green vegetable. On impulse, I threw the string bean down the hallway. Fifi raced after it, pounced on it, retrieved it and placed the string bean at my feet. Repeatedly I tossed the string bean down the hallway. Every time, Fifi retrieved it and dropped it in front of me, begging me to continue.

At first I found this game amusing, but after a while I realized that Fifi was breathing too hard. She had worked herself into a sort of frenzy. I decided it would be unkind to continue, so I refused to throw the string bean anymore, leaving it where it had fallen.

Fifi now picked up the string bean and carried it to the closet, where she placed it carefully in one of my shoes. Then she curled herself around the shoe and string bean and fell asleep, one paw on top of the string bean, guarding her treasure.

After that, whenever I prepared string beans, Fifi and I would play our game, but I always stopped before she became too agitated. And every time she would carry the string bean to one of my shoes, place it inside and fall asleep.

Brown Ants, Black Ants

Almost twenty years ago, I established a rock garden on a slope on the south side of my summer house. On the upper part of the slope I planted low-growing pines that would not obstruct the view, and to one side I placed several hemlock trees. Between pines, hemlocks and rocks I planted heather, a modest plant whose little blossoms appear early through the melting snow.

Over the years, I have added all kinds of flowers and bushes, and by now my rock garden looks as natural as if it had been there forever.

In the summer, snakes slither among rocks and plants, and chipmunks scurry from rock to rock before disappearing into a hole. Toads rest peacefully in the shade, and humming-birds dash from flower to flower.

Under one of the rocks lives a community of large brown ants. They are usually busy expanding their nest below, endlessly carrying tiny bits of soil to the surface and depositing them around the edge of the rock. One hot day in late July or early August, however, the ants became fidgety, rushing around in all directions. Their activities looked aimless, yet one sensed there was a purpose to it.

And indeed, before long they began to march along a narrow path toward a mountain laurel bush near the front door of the house. Here lay the home of small black ants.

No doubt, a brown ant on a scouting mission had discovered the nest and returned to her own nest to report the find.

Now the brown ant army arrived and began a ruthless invasion. They stole the eggs and larvae and then took the small black ants themselves as prisoners. The black ants panicked at first, often climbing to the tops of the blades of grass in order to escape. But once a brown ant touched a

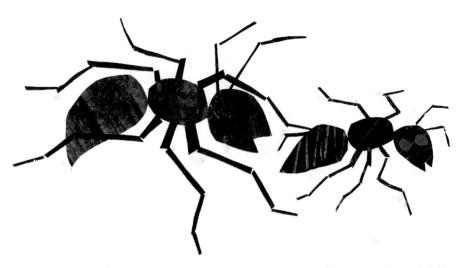

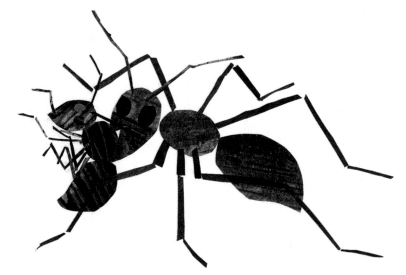

black ant, the victim surrendered without a fight and rolled itself up to be carried off in the jaws of the aggressor.

Looking closely, I noticed a two-way path: brown ants leaving their nest, and brown ants returning to their nest with the small black ants in their jaws. As they passed, they occasionally bumped into each other, then they lingered for a second or two and touched each other's antennae. Perhaps they exchanged information about their conquest.

The next day peace reigned again. The black ants' nest looked eerily empty, and the brown ants had retreated back into their home.

Several weeks later, I carefully lifted the rock where the brown ants had their nest and was surprised to see both brown and black ants living and working together. I had assumed that the black ants had become the food for their captors. But no, now both black and brown ants were equally disturbed by my intrusion and defended their castle as one. A sisterhood united!

I was intrigued enough to want to find out what was going on, so I bought a big book called *Ants*.* According to the authors, there are more than 8,800 species of ants all over the world, and, yes, some are slave masters.

However, an unanswered question remains. Year after year, the brown ants in my rock garden raid the same black ant nest near the front door. Why do the black ants in that nest not die out?

Can the brown ants really be so devilishly clever as to leave the black ant queen and a few helpers untouched so that by the following year, the brown ants are again able to conquer and enslave another generation of black ants?

* by Bert Hölldobler and Edward O. Wilson, Belknap/Harvard, 1990

Uncle Adam and His Raven

My Oma's youngest sister Liesel was married to Adam Glück (*Glück* means good luck). In his youth, before World War I, Adam had been a builder of airplanes—some flew, some never left the ground and some crashed, but he was never seriously hurt.

Whether he was inspired by the Wright Brothers' flight in 1903 at Kitty Hawk in North Carolina or whether all kinds of ideas about flying were "in the air," is hard to say. But, I am sure at that time many young people dreamed about flying machines.

In World War I, Adam had been a test pilot on the Western Front and he had many stories to tell. He met and got to know the famous flying ace: Baron von Richthofen, also known as the Red Baron. Proof of this was an old brownish photograph that hung above his bed, showing him in his flying suit with a group of flyers, among them von Richthofen. They were young, proud, and smiling. To the opposite wall of the bedroom, a large wooden propeller had been attached. During that war Adam and his planes crashed a number of times, but he survived them all in one piece, only his nose looked like an ex-prizefighter's.

When I knew Adam many years later, he owned his own small construction business. In the garden behind his house he kept a tame raven. Adam, a brusque and reticent man, would make low, soft guttural noises and the bird would cock its head, look intelligently into Adam's eyes and respond with its own soft croaks.

It was not unusual to see Adam with the black bird on his shoulder, feeding it pieces of bread and kernels of corn. Gently, ever so gently, the raven picked them out of Adam's hand. I believe that the raven's wings were clipped, but I never sensed that the bird wanted to get away.

Once, when I visited, I asked Adam how he had become the owner of a raven.

"A couple years ago I caught him in my apple orchard," he said. "Come, I'll show you how."

He crumbled up pieces of bread and soaked them in a glass filled with *Schnaps* (a kind of brandy). After the bread was drenched, he placed it into a jar, screwed on a lid and stuck it into his coat pocket. Then we walked to the apple orchard, which was about one kilometer from his house.

When we arrived, a few noisy ravens were flying in the air while others sat in the branches of the trees. Adam took the bread pieces that had been laced with *Schnaps* and scattered them on the ground.

"Now watch," said Adam, as we retreated behind a nearby tree to observe the birds.

The ravens, after first eyeing the pieces of bread suspiciously, descended, one after the other, and then began to gobble them up. It didn't take long for the *Schnaps* to take effect, and soon several birds became intoxicated. They staggered and shuffled and hobbled. And when Adam stepped forward most of them were unable to fly away.

"That's how you catch a raven!" cried Adam as he grabbed one unresisting bird. After a while Adam released the poor fellow, who hesitated, then wobbled away, looking very unhappy.

"He'll be fine in an hour or so," said Adam, and took me by the hand as we began to walk back to his house.

Suddenly I felt sorry for Adam's tame bird. I was sure Adam's raven would be happier flying with his own kind.

A Canary and a Parakeet

When I was twelve or thirteen years old we had a canary, a cheerful and lively yellow bird whose songs I loved. If he wasn't singing I'd go up to his cage and whistle. The canary would listen carefully and then respond with more of his songs.

I felt sorry for my canary being imprisoned, and whenever it was practical to do so, I opened the little door of his cage. But one day, when I had unlatched the little door, the bird flew out of his cage, *and* out of the window, which I had forgotten to shut!

For a while my canary sat in a linden tree in front of the house. I ran downstairs to the tree and called and begged him to come down. I even whistled, but he flew away and disappeared between the neighboring houses.

One flight up from where I lived with my parents lived my Opa and Oma with their unmarried daughter Helene, a shy and unassuming woman in her early thirties.

My Oma and Helene squabbled a lot.

"How come you haven't done the dishes yet?" my Oma might ask.

"Because I have a headache."

"You have a headache because you didn't get up until ten this morning."

"I slept late because I couldn't fall asleep last night."

"You couldn't fall asleep because you sat around all day doing nothing."

Then Helene would wipe away a tear and withdraw to her room as another headache made itself felt.

My Oma was usually a gentle and warm woman, but for some reason she became prickly around Helene.

I liked my Aunt Helene and often visited her in her little room. And she, too, enjoyed my company. Sometimes we played cat's cradle or checkers, or I might rummage through one of her button jars to admire the mother-of-pearl or bone buttons, while she brushed her long hair in front of the mirror. Her bureau was strewn with bottles, boxes and jars that contained perfumes, creams and powders.

"Close your eyes and open your hand," she would say, standing behind me, covering my eyes with her soft hands. Then she'd press a candy, a *Pfennig* or a bottlecap into the outstretched palm of my hand. The insides of the bottlecaps had small color photographs of famous film stars printed on them, and we children traded them the way kids in the U.S. traded baseball cards.

The day after my canary escaped I visited my Aunt Helene and explained to her how my little yellow canary bird had flown out of the window and vanished.

It was a warm day and we sat by the open window. I was sad that I had lost my bird. My aunt Helene took my hands into hers and looked into my eyes.

"Can you keep a secret?" she whispered into my ear, and I promised that I could.

"Not long ago, I met a nice man at the country fair," she said. "We danced together late into the night, and we like each other and we will get married."

She hugged me, and then, just as she let go of me, a pale blue parakeet came flying through the open window and landed on Helene's bed. Without coaxing, the bird hopped onto my outstretched finger. I carried him downstairs and put him into the empty canary cage.

Not long after that, during an air raid, a bomb exploded nearby, shattering all the windowpanes and killing my parakeet. When I returned from our air-raid shelter, I found him lying dead on the floor of his cage.

A Turtle on Elm Street

Sometimes my wife, Barbara and I like to go for a walk near our house. We cross busy Elm Street and then stroll through Smith College campus toward Paradise Park.

On one such a stroll, just as we crossed Elm Street, we saw a small turtle with yellow dots on her blackish shell ambling along the cement sidewalk.

Surely not a good spot for a turtle to be, we thought; so we decided to find a better and safer location for this reptilian. As I picked her up she quickly withdrew her head inside the shell. I carried her toward Paradise Park, a park with a river, a pond, a marsh, trees, grasses, ferns, rocks, hills and flat areas, a boathouse and even a small Japanese garden house. In the park, about one hundred yards from where we had picked up the turtle, we selected the perfect spot. It was near the river but close to the marsh, between trees and meadow, sun and shade; nearby an old rotting hollow log offered protection.

After I had set her down, her head reappeared to examine the new surroundings, but she remained in place as if to survey the new—and to us, idyllic—setting. Since the turtle wouldn't move while we watched, we continued our walk along the river path where trees hug the embankment and the branches touch the surface of the slow-moving river. At certain times of the year, pairs of ducks paddle in the water, sticking their rears up and their heads below as they look for food. Occasionally, we brought them pieces of stale bread, but they are shy and rarely accepted our offerings.

Canada geese, circling in V-formation and honking all the while, sometimes land for a stopover on a small island in Paradise Pond. This is a pond that in the cold days of winter becomes a skating rink. Then young and old, children as well as men and women, in colorful down jackets glide across the sparkling ice, some shouting and laughing, some with hockey sticks and pucks.

But today all was quiet and green and moist and warm and blooming. We met people with their dogs and greeted them with a "Hello." A boy sat on a rock at the edge of the river holding a fishing rod. A determined jogger huffed and puffed as he passed us.

We retraced our steps back to the turtle to see how she

had managed. But the turtle was gone.

We looked here and we looked there. We looked in the grass, between the ferns, under the rocks, in the water and the marsh. We searched inside the hollow log. No turtle.

In a way we were sad, but then we persuaded ourselves that she had found a peaceful and ideal place, and we continued our walk home.

On a perfectly straight line, halfway between the spot where we had picked up the turtle near Elm Street and where we had put her down in the park, we found the turtle purposefully marching toward the very same spot where we had first found her.

My wife and I looked at each other and smiled as if to say, "You can't tamper with Mother Nature."

I picked up the turtle and carried her back to Elm Street and the hard cement sidewalk where we had originally found her and set her down. Without a moment's hesitation, the turtle walked toward a bush and disappeared underneath it.

The Cat and the Owl

Sol, Linda and their daughter Anna, friends of mine, live in an apartment in New York City high above the roar of the traffic. With them lives a cat, or I should say lived a cat.

On weekends and for longer stretches in the summer, they pack their gear and themselves into their car and then they drive northward, up the Taconic Parkway. At the last exit before the toll, they turn west toward Pittsfield and the hills of western Massachusetts.

Some time ago, Sol purchased sixty beautiful acres from Harry, a short man of forty who shaved once a week. He, his round wife and two scrawny children lived in a trailer next to which a sleek powerboat stood on blocks.

Harry and his family had formerly lived in a house near where the trailer now stood, but one night during an electrical outage, he lighted a kerosene lamp that somehow caused their house to burn to the ground. In true Yankee fashion, the local townspeople collected among themselves a considerable amount of their hard-earned money and presented it to Harry to help him rebuild his house. He took the money and instead bought the fancy powerboat.

This did not endear him to the townspeople and, I suspect, he sensed the resentment and decided to move away. That is how Sol became the owner of a handsome piece of land that began at the Chickley, a fast, clean brook inhabited by trout, and ended high on a magnificent hill with a view of hills and the big sky. Sol erected a fine log cabin on top of the old stone foundation where one time Harry's house had stood.

But back to the cat. He was black and his name was Jimmy. Like Sol, Linda and Anna, the cat enjoyed the countryside. Here they all roamed among the grass, the wildflowers and the trees. Jimmy was a city cat, but he soon learned to catch mice, and to avoid foxes and raccoons. However…

Near the log cabin is an old woodshed. Here lived a large owl who watched Jimmy all summer with patience and interest. Then, one night toward the end of the season, while the unsuspecting cat slept on the steps of the log cabin, the owl struck. He swooped silently from his perch, hooked his claws into Jimmy and lifted him aloft.

My friends were awakened by horrified and plaintive meows that became fainter as the cat was carried away into the night. And then everything was quiet again.

Now my friends have a white cat. They keep a careful eye on him. So far, so good.

Wasp

Northampton, where I live, is a New England town of about thirty thousand people. Main Street starts near the railroad overpass and a large building made of yellow brick. Here Calvin Coolidge had his law office before he became first the mayor of Northampton and later the thirtieth president of the United States of America. He coined the phrase "The business of America is business," but was otherwise a man of few words, so the people called him "Silent Cal."

Main Street is about a mile long and merges into Elm Street where Smith College is located. Except for several churches, none of the buildings on either side of Main Street is higher than four or five stories; they were constructed before or right after the turn of the century.

On Main Street are a drugstore, a camera shop, a couple of bookstores, a candy shop, an optician, a bakery, a shoe store and a clothing store, an ice-cream parlor, an art gallery, a stationery store and more. Thorne's, once a department store, now is a mall housing about thirty individual stores: men's and women's clothing boutiques, a flower shop, a bath shop, a bead shop, a housewares store and a vegetarian restaurant, just to mention a few.

Lawyers, psychotherapists and all kinds of counselors have set up offices along Main Street. And I shouldn't forget to mention the courthouse, City Hall and several banks.

A delicatessen, Greek, Mexican, Italian and Indian restaurants, as well as a pizza parlor are on just one side of the block where I have my studio on the top floor of a former Army/Navy store. The Army/Navy store has been converted into an arts-and-crafts shop, one of many. Northampton is perhaps best known for its arts and crafts shops that sell ceramics, jewelry, scarves, silver buckles, leather goods, handblown glass objects and so forth.

All these different stores, the easy walking distance between them and the old-fashioned atmosphere of downtown Main Street attract people from near and far; they stroll, look and buy.

On my way to or from my studio I, too, often saunter and window-shop. One summer day, in front of Beardsley's, a restaurant, I felt something crawl across my buttocks.

42

Not giving it much thought, I reached back to brush away whatever it was. But the crawling did not subside and I slapped at it a little harder. The creeping thing, however, did not care for this and stung me. I nearly fainted! I jumped and I screamed. Now I swatted wildly at the offender, only to be repaid with a second and third sting. Whatever it was, it was *inside my pants*.

I dashed through the door into the restaurant, ran past the astonished hostess to the men's room and dropped my pants as fast as I could.

Now I was going to avenge myself! Death to the intruder!

However, my little wasp, now freed, rose from her entrapment and flew out the open bathroom window while I stood there, still dumbfounded, holding onto my trousers.

Lizards

When I was a young boy, my father and I considered our walk to *Schloss Solitude* Castle a "long" walk; it took us more than two hours to get there.

Some Sunday mornings we decided to take a "short" walk. Usually that meant we'd visit my father's parents, my grandparents.

"Don't eat too much at Grandmother's!" my mother always warned us, as we started out. She knew about my grandmother's excellent cooking and baking and that she would urge us to sample a spoonful of this and a bite of that from her Sunday meal. My mother worried that we would wreck our appetites for *her* Sunday meal, which she was preparing.

We promised not to touch my grandmother's food, kissed my mother goodbye and went our way. Soon our steps took us uphill on a dirt road. To the left and right were old stone walls, and behind them vineyards spread down toward the valley.

Approximately every one hundred yards stood simple stone structures that resembled oversized stone benches: one thick horizontal stone slab supported by two thick stone pillars. The horizontal bench part, however, was about four feet off the ground, too high to sit on.

When I had seen these stone structures for the first time, I asked my father what they were.

"In the old days, before trucks and tractors, the winegrowers carried their grapes in large wooden tubs that were strapped to their backs," explained my father.

"Whenever these men got tired, they'd place the bottom of the tub on top of the stone bench, easing the weight, and rest for a while."

These ancient stone benches were no longer in use but they still held great interest for us. Each of them absorbed the sun's heat, and the warmth attracted small green lizards, who were stretched out all over these stones to sun themselves.

One morning we made a particular effort to get there before the sun had risen too high, when the air was still cool. "Now the lizards are still sluggish and can easily be caught," my father pointed out. "But once the sun has warmed them up, they'll become very nimble. Then they'll be almost impossible to catch.

"Don't catch a lizard from behind because if you hold onto its tail, it will simply let the tail go," my father would warn me.

"In order to save its life a lizard will sacrifice its tail," my father went on. "Most of the time the tails will regenerate, grow back, but there will always be a telltale scar where the new tail starts to grow."

And indeed, looking closer, I saw one lizard with a short, stubby tail instead of a long, graceful one.

I placed my stretched-out hand a little in front of a lizard that was facing me. Slowly, ever so slowly, I moved my hand closer and closer. Then, like lightning, I cupped my hand over the little creature.

I held the lizard for a few moments. I felt it stir, absorbing the warmth of my hand, pushing its head against the inside of my hand in order to escape. Then I released the lizard and watched it disappear into a crevice at the base of the stone bench.

Never did I hurt a lizard or cause one to let its tail go. My father had taught me to be mindful and to respect these beautiful little reptiles.

When we got to my grandparents' house, we never could resist my grandmother's generous offerings. So we sampled a little stuffed cabbage, a small piece of roast beef, a spoonful of gravy and a sliver of her cherry pie, breaking our well-intentioned promise to my mother.

Nobody is perfect.

Flora and Tiger

When I was five years old, Grandmother Carle came from Germany to visit three of her five children, who lived in the United States. My father being her eldest, she stayed with us in Syracuse first.

"*Du hast Schlappohren,*" she told me as I sat in her lap. I understood but could not speak German, so I just smiled. She was right, my big ears did stick out.

After Grandmother had stayed with us for a while, she traveled to New York City to visit her son, my Uncle Hermann and her daughter, my Aunt Elsie. Elsie and her husband, Otto, were having trouble in their marriage. They had a son, Fritz, who was five years old, just my age. He was, according to Grandmother, suffering from the constant quarrels between his parents.

"You straighten out that marriage of yours," ordered Grandmother. "In the meantime I'll take Fritz with me." Which she did.

Before they departed from New York, Hermann went to a pet store and purchased a turtle as a farewell gift for my Cousin Fritz, who named it Flora. As they boarded the steamship *S. S. Berlin* in New York, Grandmother hid the turtle in her handbag and smuggled it on board. On the long journey across the ocean, the turtle was kept in the drawer of their night table. Fritz often fed and played with his new pet. But when the vessel pulled into the port of Hamburg, Flora again disappeared into Grandmother's handbag and, undetected by the immigration officers, entered Germany.

Grandmother's visit had stirred up feelings of homesickness in my mother. A year later, my parents and I also went to live in Germany.

My grandparents' garden behind their house was large, at least viewed from a child's perspective. Cousin Fritz and I often played games in this garden.

There was the henhouse with chickens and a rooster, a shed with a dozen individual pens inhabited by rabbits. Attached to that was a lean-to for a wheelbarrow, a ladder, shovels, rakes and other garden tools.

In the garden grew a cherry tree, an apple tree, a pear tree and a plum tree. Red and black currant bushes as well as gooseberry bushes thrived on either side of a paved path. Vegetables were neatly cultivated in rows. Flowers blossomed from one end of the garden to the other. And I'll never forget the sweet strawberries that always happened to be ripe on my birthday.

Between house and garden was a small paved area, room enough for a picnic table and bench.

A downspout that could be opened and closed fed rainwater from the roof of the house into a large barrel with a wooden lid. The collected rainwater, usually full of wiggly mosquito larvae, was used to water the plants during a dry spell.

All this was the home of Grandmother's Angora cat, Tiger, as well as Fritz's Flora. On sunny days Tiger would curl up and fall asleep in some corner of the garden or near the house. Pretty soon Flora would come marching along, snuggle herself close along the cat's furry belly and fall asleep, too.

The two animals had become chummy. For instance, it was not unusual to see the turtle drink milk and eat food from the cat's dish. The cat merely blinked one eye and then continued his afternoon nap.

The long-haired cat was big, fat, friendly and lazy, liked by everyone, and he in turn seemed to enjoy his simple life and the people around him.

The turtle...well, the turtle was a turtle. I was never able to figure out what went on in the turtle's head.

Every year late in autumn when the weather grew cold, Grandmother went into the garden to look for Flora. When she found her, she would talk to her for a little while and then would bury the turtle inside a wooden box filled with peat moss. Flora didn't mind; by now she had already become somewhat sleepy. The time for hibernation had

arrived and the box with the turtle inside would be stored in the cellar until next spring.

This ritual had been going on for many years. But one year, when the weather had turned cool again and it was time for Flora to be tucked away, Grandmother couldn't find the pet. She looked all over and asked the neighbors if they had seen the turtle, but she could not be found.

The following spring, when Grandfather turned over the garden with a spade, he hit what he thought was a rock. When he dug up the "rock," he discovered that it was the turtle. She had buried herself the previous fall, but had not survived the cold.

And that was the end of a beautiful friendship between Flora, a turtle, and Tiger, an Angora cat.

P. S. Oh, in case you are interested in what happened to Fritz. He stayed with his grandparents in Germany until he was twenty-one years old. He then returned to his mother in New York. To some extent his return was delayed because of the outbreak of World War II. However, I strongly suspect that Grandmother so very much loved her grandson that she invented all kinds of excuses to keep him to herself. When Fritz was finally united with his mother, they got along well with each other despite the many years of separation.

The Penguins and a Snake

When I was a young boy, I thought it was perfectly normal for a zoo to hold and exhibit animals for our entertainment and education. But now it strikes me as heartless and cruel to imprison animals, condemning them to such an unnatural and degrading existence.

Visiting the Amazon or Africa to see animals in their natural habitat appears reasonable. But how long will the Amazon jungle or the African plains remain wild and pristine when hordes of tourists flock to these places?

Let us abandon these disturbing thoughts for a minute.

Years ago, my wife and I were invited to visit a friend in Niagara, New York. We had not been there before and welcomed the opportunity to visit the world-famous falls at the border between the United States and Canada.

Less well known than Niagara Falls is a small zoo nearby. Naturally, we were attracted to it and went there. I must admit that I have forgotten most of the animals and the displays. However, one incident was unforgettable.

As we stood in front of the penguin pen, something struck me as odd. At first I was unable to put my finger on it. A weird stillness had settled over a bunch of penguins who were crowded over near one corner.

Their rigid bodies were turned toward us but their faces

50

were turned to the left, eyes fixed with an odd intensity on something in the corner. Were these real or stuffed animals? Then I began to follow their intense gaze; they all stared at exactly the same object: a smallish rock.

There! A snake!

A small green snake had curled itself up next to the rock, looking back at the penguins. It seemed just as puzzled as they were.

Snakes and penguins live in different worlds, and they were eyeing each other with great suspicion as well as curiosity. It was certainly a freak encounter, for both. I went to the zoo director and reported the odd situation.

"Ah!" he exclaimed, striking his forehead with his flat hand. "After we cleaned out the reptile enclosure a week ago, we discovered that one snake had disappeared. We looked all over, we turned the enclosure upside down but we couldn't find the little devil.

"The reptile enclosure is on a different floor and quite a distance away from the penguin pen," he said. "It's a mystery to me how the snake could get from one to the other."

Together he and I returned to the penguins, where I pointed out the snake. When the zoo director spotted the escape artist, he grinned and shook my hand.

Two Bears on 8A

Old apple trees do not grow tall and big. Instead, their main trunk becomes fat and the branches become gnarled and craggy. Here and there the bark begins to peel off and the insects start to move in to build passageways into the wood or under the bark, leaving small telltale mounds of sawdust. Moss and lichen grow on the bark and often dish-like fungi develop along the trunk, slowly draining the tree of its strength.

Yet year after year, shiny, slender new shoots emerge from the old branches to grow straight toward the sun. It seems to take forever for an apple tree to die.

Occasionally, when I walk through the forest, I will stumble upon an old, crooked apple tree with broken and dead limbs, but some of the branches still sprout leaves. Probably a long time ago, a farmer had planted this tree as a sapling in his meadow. Later the meadow was abandoned, allowing the forest to reclaim the land. Over the years oak, beech, maple and pine trees grew unchecked and engulfed the lonely apple tree, dwarfing it, but never subduing it either.

On my neighbors' land, close to the road, grow seven of these ancient apple trees. Despite their old age and the damages sustained over the years, they continue to bloom every spring and in the autumn produce small red apples. Nowadays no one picks the fruit anymore, and so the apples drop to the ground, where they start to rot. Then, all day long, yellow wasps, blue and green flies and other insects crawl over the decaying fruit to feed. At dusk or in the darkness deer, porcupines and skunks, too, come to visit and partake of the rich harvest.

After a few days in the grass, the apples begin to ferment, giving off a distinct smell, best described as sweet, sour and pungent. Fermentation is a process that turns rotting fruit into alcohol.

My wife and I had gone for a walk when we spotted a pair of brown bears, attracted by the smell of the fermenting apples, wandering down from the wooded hills. At the edge of the meadow they hesitated briefly and then trotted toward the fruit on the ground. From a safe distance we watched the bears sniff cautiously at the apples, turning them over with their paws. They began to gobble them up, munching and growling softly as they devoured the fermenting delicacy.

After the bears had gorged themselves, they appeared a little unsteady. They sat down on their rumps, but when they tried to stand on their hind legs, the bears wobbled from side to side. Their front legs, too, buckled under them when the animals wanted to walk. Soon, the bears became cross-eyed. They drooled, their tongues hanging out of their mouths.

The fermenting apples had done them in. The two bears were intoxicated!

Since moving around had become troublesome, the bears did what any self-respecting drunk would do: They stretched out and fell asleep, right there underneath the trees in broad daylight for all who walked or drove by to see.

Word of the bears' predicament reached a certain unsavory character who saw an easy opportunity to shoot a couple of bears for himself. He loaded his gun, jumped into his pickup truck and drove *north* on 8A toward his prey. Fortunately for the bears, someone had called the police and informed them of the bears' odd behavior. The police dispatched two troopers, who then drove *south* on 8A in their patrol car toward the same spot.

The would-be hunter arrived first. Gun slung over his shoulder, he approached the unsuspecting bears, but as he reached for his weapon, the police car came around the corner and stopped near the parked pickup truck.

Picture this: a beautiful late autumn morning, seven old apple trees, rotting apples in the grass, two peacefully snoring bears, one would-be hunter and two state troopers emerging from their patrol car.

The man with his gun knew right then and there that his evil plan had come to naught. He quickly retreated into his pickup truck, slammed the door and drove off.

We stayed a little longer and watched the troopers make themselves comfortable between their car and the sleeping animals, then Barbara and I turned around and headed back to our house. We were told later that the troopers stayed on to guard the bears until the sun began to set. When the bears had slept off their drunkenness, they rose up, shook themselves vigorously and ambled back to the forest. Then the two policemen climbed back into their car and drove off into the evening.

Chimney Swift

One morning during my summer vacation, when my father was home on furlough from the war, he and I went for a walk. Not far from our house we found a swift struggling on the ground, flapping its long, pointed wings against the grass. Gingerly my father picked up the bird and held it in his hand.

"Swifts are very agile birds with strong wings who spend most of the day flying in the air. It is said that they sleep while they glide through the night. But they have small, weak feet and very short legs," explained my father. "And because of that they have great difficulty taking off into the air if they fall or land on the ground." The swift remained motionless in my father's hand. Its beak was half open and it breathed in quick bursts.

"Here, you hold it," said my father, and he transferred the swift into my hand. I could feel its tiny heart pound against the inside of my palm.

"This bird has exhausted itself trying to take off," my father said.

"What are we going to do?" I asked.

"We'll let it rest for a while," answered my father. "It needs to regain its strength."

After five minutes we felt that perhaps the swift had recovered. I held the bird and lifted my arm as high as possible and gave the swift a shove, but it fell back to the ground and lay there with its wings outstretched.

"Perhaps its wings are damaged," I said.

"We'll have to take care of it," replied my father.

When we came home with the helpless swift, my mother smiled knowingly. This wasn't the first time that we had arrived with a creature in need of help. She found an empty shoe box and volunteered an old, soft piece of cloth with which to line the box.

My father placed the swift inside the lined box and slipped the lid on top. "The darkness inside the box will soothe the bird." Then he put the box in a quiet corner of the veranda, a small area off the kitchen.

The bird needed to be fed every hour or so. For that purpose we caught flies all day long. Then my father taught me how to feed the flies, one at a time, to the bird.

I held the bird in my left hand and opened its beak gently, prying it apart with thumb and index finger. In my right hand I held a fly by its wings and shoved it down the bird's throat. I waited for the fly to be swallowed, and I opened the bird's beak again. Then I dipped my little finger into a jar of water and placed a droplet inside the bird's gaping mouth. Sometimes the bird refused to close its beak, in which case I carefully forced it shut so that the drop of water would go down .

My father had told me that without water the bird would not survive. All week long I fed the bird with flies and drop-lets of water. Soon the swift got used to me, and feeding it became less of a burden. Either I got better at it or else the bird felt it could trust me.

A week later, we decided that the time had come to release the bird. My father and I climbed to the attic. I held the swift in my hand. My father opened the attic window. To the right was the church tower with its weather vane, a golden rooster; to the left we looked down onto the red roofs and chimneys of our neighbors, and beyond that were vineyards that grew toward the crest of the hill.

My father and I looked at each other; he nodded to encourage me, and I stuck my hand with the bird in it out of the window. My father smiled as if to say "Now!" and I let go.

My swift sank like a stone—but just a few feet from the ground it unfolded its wings and soared upward into the blue summer sky.

Bibliography

This is a short list of books by Eric Carle.
Only those books still readily available are listed.
If you are interested in a more comprehensive listing,
please refer to the bibliography section of *The Art of Eric Carle*.
Generally, he is both the author and the artist;
the authorship by other writers is noted.

Brown Bear, Brown Bear, What Do You See? by Bill Martin Jr 1967
1, 2, 3 to the Zoo 1968
The Very Hungry Caterpillar 1969
Pancakes, Pancakes! 1970
The Tiny Seed 1970
Do You Want to Be My Friend? 1971
Rooster's Off to See the World 1972
The Secret Birthday Message 1972
Walter the Baker 1972
Have You Seen My Cat? 1973
I See a Song 1973
Why Noah Chose the Dove by Isaac Bashevis Singer 1974
The Hole in the Dike by Norma Green 1975
The Mixed-Up Chameleon 1975
The Grouchy Ladybug 1977
Watch Out! A Giant! 1978
The Honeybee and the Robber 1981
The Foolish Tortoise by Richard Buckley 1985
The Greedy Python by Richard Buckley 1985
The Mountain That Loved a Bird by Alice McLerran 1985
The Very Busy Spider 1985
Papa, Please Get the Moon for Me 1986
All in a Day collected by Mitsumasa Anno 1986
A House for Hermit Crab 1987
The Lamb and the Butterfly by Arnold Sundgaard 1988
Eric Carle's Treasury of Classic Stories for Children 1988
Animals Animals compiled by Laura Whipple 1989
The Very Quiet Cricket 1990
Polar Bear, Polar Bear, What Do You Hear? by Bill Martin Jr 1991
Dragons Dragons compiled by Laura Whipple 1991
Draw Me a Star 1992
Today Is Monday 1993
My Apron 1994
The Very Lonely Firefly 1995
Thank You, Brother Bear by Hans Baumann 1995
Little Cloud 1996
The Art of Eric Carle 1996
From Head to Toe 1997

Special thanks to Ann Beneduce and Patricia Lee Gauch,
my good editors, for their help and patience.

ISBN 0-439-15942-3

12 11 10 9 8 7 6 5 4 3 2   4 5/0

Printed in the U.S.A.   09

First Scholastic printing, March 2000

Eric Carle's name and signature logotype are trademarks of Eric Carle.
Book design by Eric Carle and Motoko Inoue
The text is set in Walbaum Roman and Italic.
The story titles are set in Bodoni Poster Italic.